QUESTION-BASED PLANNING

**Business
Planning
Without
Mission, Vision,
Strategy, Tactics
or Objectives**

*A repentant
MBA leads a
jargon-free
revolution against
the inefficient,
ineffective, and
frustrating
tyranny of
"strategic planning"*

Derrick Van Mell

Tranton Press Books

Cover design and grids by Broadbent & Williams
Interior layout by Flying Pig Productions
Author photographs by John Devereux
Graphics by Jon Brouchoud
Edited by Barb Irvin

ISBN 0-9770914-2-2

Tranton Press Books
303 South Paterson Street
Madison, WI 53703

To Rick and Robert.
Plan ahead.

3GoodQuestions is the brand name of the author's question-based planning services. Here's what leaders have to say:

One of my managers said that with 3GoodQuestions, "Our initial 2-hour session gave us a lot of focus quickly." The website is a great tool for generating productive discussion among the managers; the outline of questions prompted us to take a few key actions right away. This is a tool CEOs of any size business would find useful.

—Jim Garner, CEO,
Sergenians Floor Coverings

3 GoodQuestions was a breath of fresh air. Their disciplined, plain English approach to business planning helped our managers focus fast on our key challenges. Getting agreement on our questions quickly got everyone working together on the big tasks for the year.

—Tom Oakley, President & CEO,
Bridge Laboratories

*E*ven though things are going very well for us and the principals have a strong relationship, Derrick's focus and discipline helped us find the time for the planning conversations we know we should have throughout the year. Using the 3GQ grid and the question-based process we quickly listed the key issues that we need to prioritize as our long and short-term goals.

—James Gersich, Partner, *Dimension IV*

*W*hen our board recommended strategic planning, I was dreading it, but 3GoodQuestions let us do everything in simple language. The questioning process naturally led us to see how all the departments inter-connect, and the benchmark goals and tasks are keeping us focused. We're already making great progress.

—Becky Steinhoff, Executive Director,
Goodman Community Center

*T*his is not about creating a big plan book that sits on the shelf. 3GoodQuestions gives each business focus by breaking things down into key problem-solving areas.

— Jeanie Farmer, Partner,
Smith & Gesteland

Question-Based Planning

TABLE OF CONTENTS

Question-based planning is

5 meetings of

2 hours each, in

5 weeks, to create a

1 page plan, with

12 monthly

90 minute progress meetings,

instead of a

2 day retreat or

5 months of analysis and

8 hours on mission and

8 hours on vision, or a

100 page binder that is

1 *expensive doorstop.*

PROBLEM

1

Can We Ever
Get Headed
In The Same
Direction?

The CEO of a mid-sized distribution company summed up what he wanted from his business plan: "I just want to get all these idiots headed in the same direction—and I'm one of those idiots! Every day, my managers come into my office, saying *their* issue is the most important thing, and I find myself saying, 'No, no, what *I'm* working on is more important!' when what we really need is a plan that gets us working together on the same things."

Now, this guy is usually soft-spoken and patient, so it startled me he used the word "idiot" in a business conversation. He was just so frustrated with planning as he'd been taught to do it.

This book exposes the problems with "strategic planning" as it's done today and provides a solution: Question-Based Planning.

Do all plans become doorstops?

A lot of management experts keep promoting a planning process that just doesn't work: their gospel is you absolutely must have a mission statement, a vision statement, strategies for this and that, tactics (are tactics just little strategies?) to support those strategies, objectives and initiatives—we all know the drill. But research shows that as many as 63% of businesses do no planning at all. So, I need to say it again: that planning process doesn't work!

This book will help you create a plan in five weeks that lets you lead your company to its goals *and* gets everyone in your shop to thank you for making their work together something special.

Do you really need to hear plans are important?

Everyone knows planning is important, so I'll be brief: *businesses that have plans make more money—and are a lot better to work at—than businesses that don't.* We all know a good plan lets you

- Remove confusion and tension about day to day tasks
- Allocate money, time, and materials efficiently
- Motivate managers by providing a clear path for growth
- Meet expectations of lenders and investors
- Anticipate risks, opportunities and change
- Allow directors to focus on high-level issues
- Allocate wealth and opportunity in a family businesses
- Show vendors, customers and advisors how they can help

How would you feel if one of your sales people told you your biggest competitor just adopted a great business plan?

What's the *one* reason plans are valuable?

Don't tell the gurus this, but few people are really motivated by money. Money is a necessity, not an inspiration. People are social, and people are kind. It's what makes us proud to be human. The root idea is that a good plan, no matter what the organization, taps the most powerful force in society: letting people work together to do something important.

What really motivates people, what everyone loves, is to do something they're passionate about and to do it with people they like to work with.

2

WHY IS PLANNING ALWAYS SO FRUSTRATING?

If planning is so important, why do we hate it so much? This chapter pulls up the "strategic planning" process by its roots.

Is planning ever easy?

No. Planning is hard because getting a group of people to agree on what's important to all of them is hard. Few people can always express themselves perfectly or read other peoples' minds.

Planning in business is hard because the issues are hard: What can our market share be in five years? Which technology will change our business most? What are our competitors up to? How will the economy treat our big customers? What's the right kind of person to hire for next year? What information helps us most? It takes time to agree on all the big questions and to really understand what they mean.

The pace of change is now so frantic that planning itself must evolve from supporting multi-year projections to energizing near-term action. This of course makes planning even harder, but a key benefit of Question-Based Planning is that it gets people thinking as a unit, able to adapt quickly to change.

Question-Based Planning doesn't make planning easy, but it does make it a lot *faster and easier*—and much more worthwhile.

*T**he primary purpose of planning is to immerse yourself in the issues***

—Richard Muther

PROBLEM	OPPORTUNITY	SOLUTION	SUCCESS

Do the semantics of strategic planning make things clear?

Of course not. Who hasn't gone nearly insane in meetings wordsmithing a "vision statement"? How is a "vision" really different from "goals"? How are strategies different from tactics? How are goals different from objectives? Is there a difference between "initiatives" and tasks? You might *think* you know what these words mean, but even if you do, you can't get six other people in a room who share the same definitions. If you're ever going to use plain English, it's in planning, when absolute clarity is so important.

The two key words in Question-Based Planning are *goal* and *task.* That's it.

Can we stay focused in a meeting more than two hours?

I doubt it. Who hasn't been mentally paralysed by a five-month "strategic planning" effort? Meeting after meeting, reams of paper, in-boxes jammed with emails. People are drained and irritated and aren't getting their work done. The other time-waster is the weekend retreat, when people really want to be with their families instead of making nice with co-workers. Even if the conversation is exciting, a week later the participants are thinking, "You know, now that I've slept on it I realize that idea was really pretty stupid" or "Gosh, I just had a really valuable idea…wish I'd thought of it during the retreat. Oh well."

People can only stay focused on a tough issue for two hours at a time, which should be the limit of any meeting. Meetings on one topic shouldn't be too close to another, otherwise the ideas don't get a chance to soak in, nor should they be much more than a week apart, otherwise people forget or lose their enthusiasm. People will only tolerate four or five meetings on one topic before expecting results. The planning schedule has to fit these basic facts of human nature.

Chapter 5 lays out a 5-week planning schedule of one 2-hour meeting each week.

Should analysis be part of planning?

No. Everyone's familiar with "analysis paralysis." It's a common and costly mistake to mix planning with analysis; the two should be kept separate. There are of course all kinds of useful analyses: market share, customer opinion, operational efficiency, industry trends, lease/own, financial performance, employee satisfaction, and on and on. But analysis should *inform* planning. Either finish the analysis a few weeks *before* the planning so everyone can absorb the information, or use the planning to uncover a need to conduct an important analysis afterwards.

What is the right role for the facilitator?

Asking good questions. Managers commonly complain that the expensive planning consultant they hired simply lectured them after spending only two days on site. It isn't enough to have good ideas; it's much more important to get everyone to really listen, participate, and agree. Every manager I talk to says exactly the same thing about the facilitator's job: "We just want them to ask good questions."

I'll have a *lot* more to say about the power of asking good questions later.

What business model should we use?

The one you've already got. If you Google images of "strategic planning diagrams" you'll see a laughable array of triangles pointing up, triangles pointing down, concentric circles, circles that overlap, and circles intersecting with spirals of different colors. Planning is hard enough, so why on earth would the facilitator also introduce a whole new way to think about your business? We've already got a well-established "model" used in 99% of the world's businesses:

Structure & Growth	Marketing & Sales	Operations
I.T.	Human Resources	Finance

It's this familiar "model" that structures Question-Based Planning.

How much consensus should we get?

A lot—among a few people, what most people call the C-Suite. Bottom-up planning usually results in no plan and a lot of disappointment. The entire staff can be involved in planning by answering a carefully crafted questionnaire or through a suggestion box, but the senior managers are the ones responsible for planning and communicating the results. They absolutely need to be headed in the same direction.

What's the connection between planning and leadership?

The plan is the practical manifestation of the leadership. A common planning problem is a leader who hesitates to commit to the calculated risks that success requires. A timid boss puts off planning to avoid contentious decisions, perhaps from a good intention for buy-in. Successful organizations have one strong leader, one who isn't primarily interested in keeping people from getting upset; but one who is deeply committed to providing everyone profoundly meaningful work.

Planning and leadership both require the ability to delegate. This means of course hiring the right managers, firing the wrong ones, and having the wisdom to know what mistakes are forgivable. The business plan must let those managers, whether of marketing or sales, HR, IT, finance, or operations, meet the plan's goals however they choose—as long as it's in a constructive, positive way.

Question-Based Planning helps you be a better leader.

What's in it for you?

A good plan is essential to corporate success, but it's also essential to your *career* success. We all know this at some level, which is why *not* having a plan (or having one no one reads or remembers) is so darn frustrating. You don't have to be the CEO to take the initiative. More on this in Chapter 4.

3

WHAT'S IN IT
FOR YOU?
AND YOU
AND YOU
AND YOU?

E ven though success depends on how much people help others, it's amazing how few managers really know how much they already help the people in the offices right next door. This will come out later in the second step of Question-Based Planning, but I've been surprised how quickly people forget the great things they've accomplished. This line of questioning lets us start Question-Based Planning in a very positive, cooperative way.

Obviously, a company succeeds if everyone does a good job, but we need to dig deeper…

How does the HR Director help the other managers succeed?

A great HR Director helps everyone by recruiting, retaining, and motivating the best people in every other department. An HR professional who knows that his or her company has a solid future and a good plan will reveal the company as a great place to work, where great managers are developed. That, too, helps everyone feel and be important.

Kahler Slater, an architecture firm in Milwaukee, has won awards as "Best Place to Work" for five years: the clients notice, which helps the marketing and sales people land more business—which keeps the CFO happy. Everyone's connected.

How does the VP of Marketing/Sales help the other managers succeed?

The obvious answer is that they provide a steady and steadily growing amount of business. But a good marketing and communications program spreads the word about the company's reputation—making the HR Director's job easy. A disciplined sales qualification process brings in the right kind of business, with friendly customers, good margins, and the technically challenging work COOs love. Good sales people also bring in all kinds of information about competitors that all the other managers can use.

PROBLEM   OPPORTUNITY   SOLUTION   SUCCESS

How does the COO help the other managers succeed?

Producing a high quality product or service is the single most important way to boost morale in an organization, which helps the HR Director. Having a reputation for working efficiently is something that all customers appreciate—and that makes the VP of Sales' job even easier. And a safe, clean, and well-organized workspace looks great when the CFO is giving the all-important facility tour to the bankers.

How does an IT Director help the other managers succeed?

Providing the right information in the right way just when it's needed is how the IT Director helps peers make successful and speedy decisions. This helps people inside and outside of the company communicate easily, which reduces friction in day-to-day decision-making. Again, everyone's connected.

How does the CFO help the other managers succeed?

Tom Oakley, now CEO of Bridge Laboratories, came up through the finance track. Years ago, when he'd just been hired as a controller with ambitions to become CFO, he told his team of accountants, "We'll know we're successful when managers come to us not just for financial reports, but for our advice on basic business decisions." Not only did he meet that goal and advance his career but also the careers of those around him.

How does the CEO help the other managers succeed?

Good CEOs don't create success; they create the conditions for success. First and most obvious, this means creating a good plan and helping the managers fulfill it. A good CEO fights for the time every week just to think about how to help everyone in the organization succeed.

A good CEO also makes sure the biggest customers are secure. They provide safe, efficient, and attractive facilities. They build goodwill in the community because a good reputation helps everyone. The CEO makes sure everyone can improve their skills, knowledge, and experience to better themselves and the company. Along with the CFO, they make sure capital for growth is at the ready. They seek out general advice and support from a board of directors or, if it's a family business, from the family council. They are the providers and storytellers. It is a difficult and lonely job, but a solid plan makes it hugely satisfying.

How do directors help the managers succeed?

Roger Axtell, who was head of Parker Pen's international marketing, special advisor to three Wisconsin governors, member of the Board of Regents for the University of Wisconsin System, trustee of the University of Wisconsin's Hospital & Clinics Authority, and author of nine books, has served on more boards than he can remember. Axtell tries to follow the advice of a Middle Ages pope who said "Examine everything, ask many questions, change little." A director who isn't asking sharp, high-level questions is probably either micro-managing or asleep.

Question-based planning helps everyone succeed together!

PROBLEM   OPPORTUNITY   SOLUTION   SUCCESS

4

How Do We Get People To The Table?

So many people have had such bad planning experiences you can't even get them to participate. I've literally heard, "If you ask me to write another mission statement, I'll kill you."

If just getting people to agree to plan is your problem, begin with diplomacy. Meet separately and informally with the five or six people you think should participate in the planning and ask them what big questions they think the business should be asking. If you've done a little homework (see www.3GoodQuestions.com), you can have some prompts ready. At the end of the meeting, ask them if it's okay to share their questions with their fellow managers.

Then compile everyone's questions on two pages and circulate them. Follow up to get their reaction and to ask, "Do you think we should get together?" That (still "informal") meeting should be just to get the conversation rolling, so start the meeting by saying something like, "Can we spend the next two hours just making sure we've got all our questions right? Later, we can decide how to answer them."

You'll see that *people find asking questions so much more comfortable than staking out and defending a position* that this won't be too hard. At the end of that meeting, when you see the energy that's being produced, you ask, "Should we use your great questions to start a new kind of plan?"

SOLUTION

5

Is There A Better Way To Plan? Yes.

Here are the steps of Question-Based Planning (QBP), each of which is described on the pages that follow. You'll see how it addresses in 5 weeks the many problems of "strategic planning" that we've just been talking about.

The readiness is all.

–William Shakespeare

PROBLEM   OPPORTUNITY   SOLUTION   SUCCESS

Week 1: Organize simply to plan efficiently

Who should participate?

The CEO should participate in all the key meetings, and if you're organized like every other business in the world, the team sitting around the planning table should also include:

VP of Marketing	VP of Sales
COO	HR Director
CFO	IT Director

Of course, sometimes the titles differ by industry; sometimes people wear two hats. If you work in a hospital, you might include a trustee, the Medical Director, or Chief Nursing Officer.

Any more than this and you can't get a good conversation going. This is the leadership team, so let them lead. The planning process shouldn't be distorted just to make people feel important. Chapter 4 answered the question, "How do we get people to the table?" if you're stuck.

*T**he plan is nothing. The planning is everything.***
—President Dwight D. Eisenhower

How should we run the meetings?

All meetings are strictly two hours. More, and everyone will get resentful. Having the discipline to start and stop on time conveys seriousness and respect. Meetings should be a week apart so ideas can sink in but not be forgotten. Each of the five meetings described in this chapter require a small amount of preparation and follow-up. The facilitator will handle those emails.

Who should run the planning?

It's almost always best to have an outsider, for their objectivity, freshness, general business skill, and maturity. Remember what everyone says? "We just want someone who asks good questions; we don't want someone telling us what to do." No one wants a lecture.

How much consensus should we try to get?

Some companies want everyone to participate, but most people would rather follow a good leader than be one. It's important not to confuse consensus with communication. It is a great help to planning, however, to have an active "suggestion box" as a source of ideas; it's also important to communicate the plan clearly and often, once it's done.

What does the end product look like?

It's one page and you can see a sample on page 33.

What time of year should we plan?

If you don't have a plan, the time is now. Planning every year or just after some major change is sensible.

PROBLEM OPPORTUNITY SOLUTION SUCCESS

Outline all the big questions (also Week 1)

The CEO of a large IT development firm would let people in her meetings brainstorm ideas for half an hour and then would gently ask, "What are the questions we're trying to answer here?" She'd write those questions down and then turn her notepad around and ask, "Does this seem right?" Every time, we'd not only agree with the questions but, more important, realize we knew the answers—and feel like *we* were the geniuses!

It was experiences like this that inspired me to create Question-Based Planning.

Traditional "strategic planning" starts with the hardest part: listing everyone's big goals in some agonizing mission or vision statement. Imagine starting by brainstorming together all your company's big *questions* instead. Since the time of Socrates, we've heard why asking questions is good for developing ideas. Asking questions is a better way to start business planning because it

- Doesn't force people to stake out *positions*
- Lets people test ideas with others
- Helps everyone understand everyone else's points of view
- Doesn't force people to answer before they've thought about it
- Gets people thinking about things outside their "silos."

You've already seen the basic part of the grid on the next page, the universal business "model." I've added here six of the most basic topics for each. At www.3GoodQuestions.com clicking any of the 36 topics reveals 3 good questions in the top box. You can project this on the wall to prompt the planning team's own great questions *and* to let everyone see how they connect. It's positive, productive, and enjoyable.

The "game" of coming up with questions is so much more positive and productive than debating "strategies" that you'll find it hard to stop. The facilitator shouldn't yet allow people to spend time answering the questions. That's in week 4.

Facilities (More)

1 How do our location, design, and facility financing support our mission and operations?
2 How does our facility tour help us sell? Where is it weakest?
3 Should we lease or own for the next five years? Afterwards?

Structure & Growth	Marketing & Sales	Operations
Purpose & position	Brand & marketing plan	Work process
Business plans	Market research	Job design
Family business	Communications & PR	Quality
Mergers & acquisitions	Internet/websites	Innovation
Facilities	Customer relations	Purchasing & inventory
Industry specialists	Sales management	Supply chain & logistics

I.T.	Human Resources	Finance
IT planning	Leadership	Analysis & financial planning
Software	Compensation	Financing & fundraising
Intranet	Diversity & compliance	Reporting & tax planning
Hardware & systems	Organization & culture	Wealth management
Security	Retention & recruitment	Risk management
Telephones & other devices	Training & development	Succession & exit planning

© 2007 Derrick Van Mell

LOG IN I PRINT ALL QUESTIONS I ABOUT US I CONTACT US

www.3GoodQuestions.com is, of course, clickable.

PROBLEM ● OPPORTUNITY ● SOLUTION ● SUCCESS ○

Week 2: Ask the 3 departmental questions

These are separate 2-hour meetings with each of the department heads (the planning team) and a few of their staff. All the preparation needed is to email these 3 questions in advance and to ask the participants to jot down their notes.

1. What are your proudest accomplishments of the past 2 years?

It's amazing to me how quickly people forget the great things they've done. By hearing how people describe what they've accomplished and seeing the pattern of issues, the facilitator learns the style and strengths of the departments.

2. What are your biggest challenges over the next 2 years?

Most people already know what's important and what needs to be done. It helps if the facilitator is an expert—or brings along an expert—in that particular department, to stimulate thinking, contribute ideas, and be able to report to the leader any departmental adjustments that might be needed.

3. What are your most important tasks for the next 12 months?

By having in front of you the 2-page outline of all the big questions, the departments can create a long list of the tasks they think are most worthwhile. They should be grouped as high, medium and low priorities.

PROBLEM   OPPORTUNITY   SOLUTION   SUCCESS

Thomas Jefferson once said, I've noticed that the harder I work, the luckier I get. *This is also true for planning as a group. A good plan attracts new ideas and opportunities like a magnet, but it takes hard work from everyone in the organization and attention to detail. A good plan creates something bigger and more powerful than the sum of each individual contribution.*

Week 3: Ask the 3 keystone questions

Now you'll have the outline of the big questions and great ideas from each department. The planning team will have had a week to absorb and sift through (perhaps subconsciously) what's important. They'll then be ready to tackle the 3 tough, keystone questions:

1. How do we compete today—really?

Provide facts, not wishful thinking. To say, "Our quality is the best" or "With our customer service" is pointless, unless you've got a fact, like awards won or a unique training program. Businesses compete by having a unique product (patent protected) or a stranglehold on some channel of distribution. This discussion might make you realize that with a little effort you can nail down a great differentiator—which becomes a task to put in your plan.

2. What does the future hold?

Competition, regulation, demographics, technology, and staffing can hold risks and opportunities, but business is about accepting risks, so don't waste time on issues with low probabilities or little consequence. Like the goals, ideas for tasks that reduce risks and capture opportunities will emerge naturally from the discussion of these questions.

3. What do we want to be remembered for?

No one wants to be remembered just because they made a lot of dough. People do want to be remembered for how they made the world a better place, bringing us back to the core reason for planning: helping people work together to help other people. Here, the leader should listen carefully to what everyone says, but it's up to him or her to capture the inspiring essence. It can help to get a professional writer to suggest some alternatives.

PROBLEM   OPPORTUNITY   SOLUTION   SUCCESS

"This is why we want people to remember us..."

Nuts and bolts manufacturer
We make machines and structures strong and safe.

Bank
We help leaders put our depositor's money to good use in our community.

Hospital
We keep families healthy, happy, and strong.

Accounting firm
Providing the facts for life's most important financial decisions.

Candy store
We provide a small pleasure in a big way.

School
We help kids make good decisions for the rest of their lives.

Business planner
We help people enjoy accomplishing great things together.

Biotech
Helping develop effective and affordable medicines.

Flooring distributor
We provide our retailers the products and value their customers love.

Week 4: Create a long list of goals and tasks

At this point, the planning team now has great material to work with to create a long list of goals and tasks:

- The outline of all their important questions
- Ideas about the challenges and tasks in each department
- Ideas about competitiveness, the future, and their purpose.

This step of Question-Based Planning is strenuous, but the participants will know they're going to be able to sleep on it for a week. Pages 30 and 31 suggest ideas about the types of goals and tasks that work.

This week is also a good time for each senior manager to take two hours outside of work to reflect on their personal goals. If you're unclear about your goals for your family, community and spiritual life, how can you commit fully to a goal in your business? Three important personal questions related to business planning are:

1. How is what I *need* to earn different from what I *want* to earn?
2. How would I rebalance my time inside and outside work?
3. Can this become the place I want to work for ten more years?

PROBLEM   OPPORTUNITY   SOLUTION   SUCCESS

Confirm the leader's direction

Also during this week, the 4th in Question-Based Planning, the leader needs to review this long list of goals and tasks to make sure it's headed in the right direction. The leader also needs to identify the one powerful goal that will pull all the rest along with it.

It's tough being a leader and one of the toughest parts of the job is to set goals that make employees uncomfortable. The leader might ratchet goals up or down or impose a goal or task no one really wants. But the leader who tries to please everyone of course pleases no one.

A good plan gives you the courage to say no and the courage to say yes. It means giving up good ideas because they don't fit the plan. It might mean having to face that some manager will never support the plan and should work elsewhere. Planning and leadership require the honesty to admit one's mistakes. They highlight the leader's ability to make hard decisions without perfect information.

A good plan reduces tension by pointing people in one direction.

*T**he primary characteristic of a leader is courage,
for without courage, nothing becomes possible.***
— Winston Churchill

PROBLEM OPPORTUNITY SOLUTION SUCCESS

Shared goals get managers headed in the same direction

Goals should of course be challenging, measurable, and inspiring. There shouldn't be too many of them. Above all, goals should lead managers to work together.

Margins, not sales: A common goal is "Double sales in 3 years," but it implies everyone can sit around waiting on the sales department. Consider instead a common goal of "Increase gross margin from 27% to 37%." This gets every department involved.

Efficiency: Another version of the gross margin goal is a shared goal of efficiency, measured in total cost per unit produced.

Customer relations: The measure of customer relations is repeat business. Few things are as satisfying, or as efficient as growing your business through existing relationships.

Quality: Few things build pride more than a quality product or service. I'm sure you can find a suitable measure for your industry. The business schools and press deserve a lot of credit for getting people to see how everyone contributes to quality.

Culture: If you've got a positive culture with a reputation for being a great place to work, the first measure of success is turnover. Other goals could be time to hire or participation in the suggestion box.

Wouldn't you feel great if your team had one page of goals like this?

Shared tasks toward common goals

Once the goals are set, it's much easier to agree on the right tasks:

One company had a gross margin goal to reduce direct costs and another goal to foster a cooperative small business culture. Since this company had 157 employees, they set a shared task of: "Get 157 cost savings ideas by September 30." Using the same number as the head count reinforced the goal of company-wide involvement.

The task list in your plan should be realistic, yet challenging. Tasks should be listed in a sensible sequence and led by one person responsible for a cooperative effort. There are few things as satisfying as checking off accomplished tasks as the months go by.

The "semantics" of Question-Based Planning are goal and task. Not mission, vision, strategy, tactics, or objectives.

Week 5: Refine goals and set the year's tasks

In this, the final 2-hour meeting, the managers talk through the long list of goals and tasks and, thinking about what's important and what they have time for, boil it down into one page.

The facing page is an example of the result. It has at the top the answer to the 3rd keystone question, "What do we want to be remembered for?" (Some people would call this your mission, the least objectionable word in the "strategic planning" lexicon.)

This one page looks simple, but you now know it reflects an enormous amount of careful thought by a lot of smart people. This kind of planning takes some getting used to, as we're so accustomed to fat planning binders and fancy words that don't mean much.

This plan won't be perfect. You'll have missed something, and you'll want to tweak it right away. Some managers might want to ignore it because it puts everything out into the open. Tell yourselves that you simply won't change the plan for 3 months—by then you'll see it starting to pay off:

- People working together on important things
- Progress toward your goals
- A feeling of focus, confidence, and pride

It won't be long before you'll want to share your plan with the whole staff, your banker, and key customers and vendors. Don't worry that you're exposing your weaknesses: instead, you'll impress everyone who can help you that you've got the honesty, brains, and courage to get better and better.

2008 business plan

We help the best food wholesalers in the US create packaging that improves every customer's shopping experience.

Primary goal
Increase Gross Margin to 33% by year end

Revenue goals
1. Open the Northwest sales territory with $XX million by 3QTR.
2. Increase backlog by 25%.
3. Increase client satisfaction ratings quarterly.
4. Increase repeat business to 70%.

Efficiency and quality goals
5. Increase units per hour by 10%.
6. Reduce rejection rate below 0.25%.
7. Increase inventory turns of raw material to 8 and WIP to 10.

Overhead goals
8. Foster a small business culture at each site.
9. Maintain administrative payroll at 15% of revenue.
10. Reduce voluntary turnover to 25%.

Tasks
- Specify and budget the ERP — 02/29/08 — Jim
- Brainstorm 200 cost savings ideas — 02/29/08 — Jim
- Launch employee recognition program — 02/29/08 — Joe D.
- Identify and "un-sell" lowest 15% of customers — 03/31/08 — Helen
- Create a corporate facility plan — 03/31/08 — Derrick
- Redesign and launch intranet — 05/31/08 — Patrick
- Decide whether to pursue Canadian business — 05/31/08 — Helen
- Establish goals for the South and East regions — 07/31/08 — Joe O.
- Create high-level process flow diagrams — 07/31/08 — Jim
- Recruit advisory board — 08/31/08 — Joe D.
- Launch new brand campaign — 08/31/08 — Helen
- Launch first employee satisfaction survey — 12/31/08 — Joe D.

Updated February 10, 2008

PROBLEM   OPPORTUNITY   SOLUTION   SUCCESS

Schedule progress reviews every month

This is an obvious step, but you need religion about it. As tasks are done and goals are met, the team should add or change them depending on how much time and money they've got. The first few meetings might be bumpy, because previously planless managers are used to coasting through progress reviews. However, in time and with a strong facilitator, people will learn it's much more satisfying to report on their own contribution than to avoid responsibility.

CEOs who report to a board should make the progress report a standing agenda item. This keeps the directors comfortable that things are on track and keeps them out of the managers' hair.

The entire planning process should be repeated every year, or sooner if there's some gigantic change. Keep track of all the tasks that have been done: it becomes a record for next year's planning and a source of pride.

*B**e sure that you're right. Then go ahead.*
—Daniel Boone

PROBLEM   OPPORTUNITY   SOLUTION   SUCCESS

*M*ake no little plans. They have no magic to stir men's blood and probably themselves will not be realized. Make big plans; aim high in hope and work, remembering that a noble, logical diagram once recorded will never die, but long after we are gone will be a living thing, asserting itself with ever-growing insistency. Remember that our sons and grandsons are going to do things that would stagger us... Think big.

—Daniel Burnham

SUCCESS

6

How Will We Know We've Been Successful?

A good plan fits on one page. It starts with one key goal that's memorable and snaps everything into focus. It also includes five or six other shared goals and lists the exciting tasks which, as they are accomplished over the next twelve months, help everyone work together toward their goals. While a jargon-packed "strategic plan" might seem more important, it's only superficial. A real plan is straightforward and clear.

You know a business plan is working when you see it pinned to walls throughout the building. You'll know it's working because everyone knows what's in the plan, and they like to talk about it. You'll know you've got a successful plan when you realize you don't have a problem with office politics, a symptom of planless drift. To risk the obvious, you'll know you're successful when you see yourselves succeeding!

The most powerful result of planning is the intense satisfaction you'll feel when you see your co-workers enjoying working together, doing something great, something they'll be proud to be remembered for.

I sincerely hope Question-Based Planning will help you give everyone you work with the profound personal and professional rewards of working together, accomplishing great things.

—Derrick Van Mell

PROBLEM   OPPORTUNITY   SOLUTION   SUCCESS

About the author

Derrick Van Mell developed Question-Based Planning and www.3GoodQuestions.com to provide leaders a better way to provide their organizations the direction and clarity they need to do great work together.

Derrick is Principal of Van Mell Associates, which he founded in 1991. In addition to business planning, Van Mell Associates (www.vanmell.com) provides planning and project management for buildings for business.

Derrick and his team bring different experiences and perspectives to bear on their clients' issues. Derrick lectures at home and abroad, and he is the author of the book *Buildings Matter* and dozens of articles. He has a B. A. in economics from Tufts University, an MBA from Loyola University and an M. A. from Northwestern University. He is married and has two children.

Derrick Van Mell
(608) 260-9300
derrick@vanmell.com